Creme De La Crematorium

MALCOLM SAXTON

authorHOUSE®

AuthorHouse™ UK Ltd.
500 Avebury Boulevard
Central Milton Keynes, MK9 2BE
www.authorhouse.co.uk
Phone: 08001974150

First published by AuthorHouse 10/23/2008

ISBN: 978-1-4389-0902-8 (sc)

Printed in the United States of America
Bloomington, Indiana

This book is printed on acid-free paper.

Dedication

This book is dedicated in loving memory of FRIEDERIKE INGEBORG ISERMEYER, my lovely wife. With my grateful thanks for all of her loving devotion to me during my `stroke` and for her endless encouragement of my career as a WRITER. Friederike Darling. Words are not and never can be enough! Rest in peace , and I'll see you in the morning.

I cannot let this opportunity pass without mentioning my best friend Peter Ernst Rudolph Klahn.

Whose help and encouragement to me both in our native Germany and here in England has been beyond measure. Peter, I GREET YOU WELL!

Finally, to Thandi, without whom I can achieve nothing. I love her more than life itself

Her part in my life is beyond estimate or calculation Thandi, I Love you. Please marry me and SOON!

P.S. to David Nathan, arts writer at the Jewish Chronicle for suggesting the title. You see David, I DID listen. Reader, Many and varied have been the characters you have met in this book. All of them are, or were real living loving laughing crying people. Likewise the events described were real, I WAS THERE! THEY HAPPENED TO ME!

Of Red Knob no more was seen or heard nor indeed was any news sought. Jim my great friend and mentor I miss to this day. He and Harry have both been called to the Grand Lodge Above where doubtless they find themselves frequently convulsed with laughter at the continuing idiocy of the Church of Englands' ministers Jim used to say" they're as camp as a row of tents; queers every last one of them!"

Creme De La Crematorium

Black Monday in the City of London was a Black day indeed, for thousands of people in thousands of ways. For myself it meant the end of my job; the end of my "fat cat" salary, end of my lavish expense account and the end of a very satisfying lifestyle of comfort and luxury. What was I to do? What could I do? I was trained as an Organ Scholar at Rochester Cathedral; completing my education at Jesus College Cambridge. For most of my life I had been a music Professor; but now what? That was the question.

First I had to get home and do some serious thinking. I was allowed to enter my office where some 'sycophantic ass licker' had emptied my desk placing my things in a plastic rubbish bag. Lifting the bag onto my back I walked into Moorgate like a Summertime Santa Claus en route to London Bridge station. Before boarding a homebound train I made a few telephone calls. As always my wife Friederike suggested what turned out to be the answer to my problem "Max they are wanting an organist at the Crematorium" You can do that and make some money while you wait for something better"

Settling myself behind my study desk I telephoned the Superintendant of the crematorium. He spoke very promisingly and arranged that I should call upon him on Friday afternoon. Much heartened I prepared myself for the interview.

Graham Liniment, the Superintendant turned out to be an avuncular young man who had lately suffered the double whammy of being turned down for the monastic life by the Catholic Church and had suffered a heart attack. We very slowly climbed the stairs to the Organ gallery where stood the newly installed organ smelling strongly of bees wax . Opening up the console I turned on the power and selecting some soft stops I began a celestial sounding improvisation on the Catholic hymn Vexilla Regis. Graham then asked me for something a little more strident saying" What will it do?" Thumbing the Full Organ piston and pressing the full Pedal toe piston I launched into a performance of the Final from the Organ Symphony No.1 by Louis Vierne.

At the completion of this piece we were joined by a very tall immaculately dressed man in a black jacket and formal striped trousers who warmly shook my hand saying "ALLO BRUVVAH" This turned out to be The Chapel Master, one Jim Rivers. "Just you remember Professor that hi am the Chapel Master 'ere, not that fat prat, EE don't know fuck all about fuck all ee don't I calls 'I'm Red Knob" Really Jim" I SAID WHY Red Knob? "COSEES A TIGHT FISTED WANKER"

On more than one occasion Jim proved to be *my Saviour.*

"Nah Professor, we need you on Monday at 1O'clock, OK?"

This was my first engagement and I WOULD BE PAID` got sei Gedank`

"I suggests as'ow you get 'ere at nine o'clock like" said Jim. "So I can show you the ropes like". On the Monday I arrived as Jim had suggested and we went up into the organ gallery. "Ave

look at your prezzie from Uncle Graham, Professor" said Jim, a closed circuit television monitor was mounted onto the top of the console, "this allows me to monitor the progress of the cortege, see the hearse entering the crematorium grounds; when they pull up outside the chapel;

and when they carry in the body and place it on the Catafalque". "That little lot Professor costs me and Arry our bonuses this year, like I said, 'ees a tight fisted Wanker" said Jim with great feeling. "Watch what happens on this next one Professor to get your eye in like" Said Jim. I saw the hearse approaching through the gates; saw it draw up outside ; saw the bearers carry the body to the catafalque and settled back to listen to the service.

After the usual banal claptrap that the Church of England Ministers spiel off, we came to the committal. This is where the minister presses a red button which causes the centre part of the catafalque to descend. Some relatives at this point rush to the catafalque to say a few valedictory words.

And so it proved in this case. <u>AN OLD LADY WHOM I TOOK TO BE THE WIDOW HOBBLED UP TO THE CATAFALQUE AND IN A VOICE QUAVERING WITH EMOTION SHE SHOUTED</u>" Bye, Bye 'ARRY YOU 'AD a lovely big Knob I WILL Always remember Yer" A this point I had to stuff my handkerchief in my mouth to prevent my laughter from becoming audible.

Now approached the Hearse and four cars of the funeral which I was to play for, I turned on the telly and saw the Cortege sweep around the large circular lawn, to pull up outside the chapel. I started playing 'Solemn Melody' by Walford Davies as the bearing party conveyed the body to the catafalque. They saluted and departed and the service began with the hymn The day Thou gavest Lord is ended. All seemed in order until I looked down to the catafalque. In a spine chilling moment realised that all was far from well.

The body had not been pushed far enough onto the catafalque leaving the head of the coffin resting on the outer rim so that on descent the lower part of the coffin would go down, leaving the head to as it were catch up. I could bear to look no further. The next hymn was announced and the moment of truth could be deferred no longer. The congregation was asked to stand and I saw the minister's hand move to the red button and the flowers on the coffin lid shook as the coffin began to descend, and then CRAAASSSHH! AND ALL HELL BROKE LOOSE

The front row of mourners charged up to the catafalque led by a large man in a tight blue suit. He looked over the catafalque and surveyed the carnage below. He turned and rushed to confront the Vicar,"VIS IS ALL YOR FAULT YOU SILLY BORN BASTARD he screamed: " YOU'VE UPSET MY MUVVER Y OU 'AVE" promptly punching the Vicar's nose. Men shouted and swore most horribly; women screamed and fainted.

At this juncture enter Jim complete with a cup of tea and a glass of Brandy I had increased the power of the organ in order to drown the worst of the screams and the foul language and then Graham appeared flapping his arms like a demented Walrus and saying please, please. Jim with his cup of tea and his bottle of Brandy had the situation under control very swiftly; 'ere yar my old mate' he said to Blue suit: " git that dahn yor froa'and you'll feel better like, losing your Farvie is an 'ard business init". Jim complete with his teacup sat down with the Widow, put his arm around her and said "Never you mind daahlin' 'ee ain't far orf and you'll see 'I m agen like, trust me. Result peace all round and hysterical laughter at Jim's parody of Graham flapping his flippers and pleading for calm.

As I climbed into my car to drive home I could hear Jim singing "WHEN YOU COME TO THE END OF A PERFECT DAY.

Day Two The Indian Love Call

I arrived at the console and prepared for the first job of the day. Psalm 23 and Abide with me Piece of cake or as Jim would and did say "Piece of Piss Professor and so it turned out. Then I became aware of Jim sitting next to me on the organ stool. "You got any fink more 'ere today Professor?" No Jim, I said the next one is an Indian one so my services are not required. "Professor my old dahlin'hi can tell you as 'ow your services are fuckin' required, A've a butchers at 'im wots dahn vair"

Gazing down towards the catafalque I saw the largest coffin that I have ever seen."Jew know 'ow much that geezer weighed in life?" asked Jim, I shook my head. "50 bleedin' stone that's all" said Jim. "Nah Professor I'm a big bloke, but I ain't no CHILES ATLAS or nuffink (He meant Charles Atlas). "Me and 'Arry are going to need your elp pullin im on and pushin im in like, so come dahn below and we'll show you ow like"

I somewhat reluctantly followed Jim and Harry to the furnace room. "Nah", said Jim, when the bell goes you know that the cawfin's at grahnd level" "You and 'Arry then pulls it onto my trolley and push it to the mouft of the furnace like and then we 'as to push very ard You gotta push like yor pushin' a BLACK MAN ORFT YOR MUVVA!" The bell sounded and Harry and me approached the huge coffin.

Gingerly we began to pull this Leviathan towards the rollered trolley which was being held ready by Jim and a gravedigger. Gently but firmly we coaxed the coffin onto the trolley. With a nervousness beyond imagination we wheeled the coffin to the closed mouth of the furnace. Lining it up Jim said "Nahven gents we all gotta be well be'aved 'cos we are bring watched by the family from the viewing room"

"Why does they do that for, Jim" WAILED Harry

"They does it HARRY BECAUSE Johnnie Indian over the years 'as formed the opinion as how that people what works 'ere are a bunch of light fingered bastards who will lift off the lid of the coffin and 'elp themselves to all 'is JOOLS an' that. So they wants to see the box

11

well alight like". The bell eventually rang and Harry, Jim and I positioned ourselves for the big push. "AWRIGHT MATE?" a roar from Jim and a thumbs up sign and then "Right then push you bastards" and we were off. The great coffin rolled into the furnace and at last the shout from Jim "AWRIGHT MATE" and we could let go and relax. As we ascended the staircase I said to the others let's go to the Tigers Head for a pint. "Bleedin' good idea Professor" said Jim, the pub here is comfortable but the beer that they sell here is a load of old AUSPICE". Arriving at the Tigers Head, we settled into the Private bar.

"Professor, Can I ask you a personal question like?" asked Jim

"Ask away Jim" I said

"Well nah PROFESSOR my old dahlin' would I be right in finkin that you are of the Hebrew persuasion like? said Jim. Laughed" "You are asking if I am a Jew'?

"The answer is yes, Jim but why do you ask

"Becorst Professor my old china, next week we 'ave a forbytwo funeral in 'ere and the funeral director can't find no Rabbi to say the Kaddish like, they pay well and if you want to wash the body and do the shrouding up like; he'll give you two 'undred and fifty quid like".

"Kaddish no problem Jim" I said;"But washing and shrouding is not really my thing".

"Awright" said Jim, I shall tellem that you will do the Service but like you ain't too keen on the washin' and shroudin'like".

AND SO my new company which I named GREEN PASTURES was born.

I could surely do a better job than your average Church of England Parish Priest. In fact it always amazes me, that a seeming never ending stream of daft buggers descend into this haven for the FAMILY FOOL. Green pastures has become extremely popular with ordinary folk or what the Parish Priest calls the Common People. So much, so that my activities have earned my EXCOMMUNICATION from the church.

I am no longer allowed to enter my Parish Church in order to pray or to worship. I cannot receive the Sacrament nor is any Lay Member of the church allowed to visit me with the Sacrament. All this on the orders of THE DIOCESE!! From what one reads in the more popular Sunday Newspapers Parish PRIESTS SHOULD BE ENCOURAGED TO NOT ONLY WEAR THEIR COLLARS BACK TO FRONT BUT

THEY SHOULD WEAR THEIR TROUSERS BACK TO FRONT ALSO.

"Nancy boys" anyway, most of them are. I was chosen to officiate at the funeral of JOE STRUMMER. Joe Strummer band known as The Clash I WAS AUDITIONED FOR THIS JOB and was successfully chosen, not wished on the grieving family by a funeral arranger who was scared into recommending the PARISH PRIEST by an intimidating RURAL DEAN. Rural Dean; the term always reminds me of a irascible old man I a mud stained suit held up by a length of baling twine.

The Nuclear Hexplosion!

It started as a peaceful day at the crematorium, boring almost. The first four funerals having Psalm 23 to the tune of "Crimond followed in each case by "Abide with me". Lunch time arrived and, taking my Marmite sandwiches I walked along to the fishpond and sitting on a park bench I sat soaking up the sunshine. Hearing a rustling in the bushes opposite I looked up to see a long raking snout protruding. I t was our tame fox "Fred, come for his slice of sandwich. Cemeteries and Crematoria are becoming wild life sanctuaries. We regularly see a family of badgers traipsing home to bed. Foxes and a plethora of wild birds all of which is fascinating. I eventually returned to my place at the console of the organ in order to play th the remaining funerals that afternoon. I sat at the console working on an improvisation on the catholic hymn"Condito r alme siderum.Suddenly B A N G !

Speaking As one who has survived two bombs in my time spent in Tel Aviv and in Jerusalem and been road mined on the Nablus road in the Negev desert I can assure you that I know a bomb when I hear one.

All the lights went out on the console as the organ died under me. A great rush of air which smashed several windows, various inarticulate sounds and Jim' great roar of "What the fuckin 'ell was that/ Remembering my training from the Army of ISRAEL I rolled off the console onto the floor and crawled under a pew.

Eventually I heard footsteps on the gallery stairs and Jim's voice

"You alright there, Professor.? I assured Jim that I was shaken but not stirred"

"Wots ; appened dahn vair Professor is summfink wot you don'twanter know abaht"said Jim.

That geezer who you played for at ten o' clock ad got a bleedin' pacemaker wot they'd left in' is body. Them fings is radio active Professor"SO when me an'Arry frows 'im in the furnace like it gets to two fahsend degrees centigrade and goes off like, It blew the lot to fuck, the bloke, 'is cawfin, the cremator everyfink.!

"Me an; Arry gets called to the office and Red knob says "Can you two get on your gardening uniforms, and when the furnace has cooled somewhat, climb in and scrape what you can from the interior so that you can later recremate this poor man's remains? "Now professor 'Arry is not a well manEe dont't like black cars , or wreaths, or cawfins or nuffink like that an' 'is nerves is shot to shit anyroad, so by the time Red knob 'as finished 'Arry is crying and shakin; and that,

"So I say RED KNOB, "Wot you are harskin uis a very, ard task so can me an"'Arry, ave a bottle of brandy to keep our spirits up like?

"Red knob puts on 'is "holy face "Really Jim I think to take Alcohol in the face of death would be unseemly"I says well yo'ure well named as Red knob you tight fisted wanker and then dear old 'Arry poor old 'Arry wot never says boo to a goose pipes up wit Yer Thank you Virgin"

"graham, wots an ardent Catholic says "Really Harry why are you invoking the VIRGIN? "TO which 'Arry says "Cos you're a tight CUNT.

The Chinese Chop

My next request came from a shop which had a Chinese gentleman to be buried.

Can you speak Cantonese" Asked the lady funeral arranger?

"Not a word I replied, with me it's German or nothing".

She and I agreed that I should visit the family and arrange for the eldest daughter to translate. I would speak slowly and loudly in English, allowing her sufficient time to translate before proceeding with the Eulogy.

That all seemed agreed until an elder brother arrived on the scene. Staring at me, he pointed at me and began to scream at the top of his voice I thought ALLO!"I'm going down like a lead balloon with one hung low here!"Fortunately the daughter was powerful enough a figure t0o control the situation and I left the house promising to type out every word of the Eulogy which, after translation could be circulated to the principal mourners so that they might follow the proceedings.

The day of burial arrived and I entered the chapel in the undertakers shop to find my translator and her brother engaged in fisticuffs! It turned out that the girl was a high ranking officer in the Police force and knew how to defend herself.

Onehanglow lay in his coffin with his glasses on. We all arranged ourselves around him and off we jolly well went I did the agreed "spiel" and many others uttered what seemed like well chosen words. On went the lid of his coffin; we carried one hung to the hearse, loaded him in and set off for the cemetery. I WAS SITTING NEXT TO THE DAUGHTER IN THE LIMOUSINE but during the journey noticed that she was throwing what appeared to be toffee papers out of the car window.

Finding a small plastic bag in my pocket I proffered it to the daughter. She shook her head vigorously "You know, understand Johnnie "she said these papers are prayers to confuse the devil" "He follow papers and not attack my father's soul"!

ARRIVING IN THE GRAVEYARD WE PULLED UP AT THE APPOINTED GRAVE. Out got the family and busied themselves erecting a small picnic table on which they placed two bottles of Saki and a freshly cooked chicken, some apples and oranges were tastefully arranged and then a large brass urn was produced and a large quantity of devil money was burnt! I was at the time seriously skint so it all seemed anathema to my Jewish nature!

The body was conveyed to the grave and an immense number of joss sticks were waved around. It was during this that my attention was drawn to a large brown swiftly moving shape, as a LARGE DOG FOX DARTED FROM AN ADJACENT GRAVE, GRABBED THE FRESHLY COOKED CHICKEN, SWUNG IT over his back and was off like a Jewish foreskin . Utter pandemonium; as all of the mourners and family gave chase. screaming blue murder' The fox, utterly unmoved by the commotion., made good his escape over the wall and into the next field. A younger brother was ordered with many screams and cuffs about the head to go to the local 'chippie' to try and replace the stolen food. HE ARRIVED BACK TO MORE CUFFS Brandishing a

The Human Torch

I drove into the grounds of the crematorium
to commence my organ playing duties

Getting out of my car, I saw Jim advancing
towards the rose garden with a fork, a hammer
and

"What on earth has happened here" Jim
binding twine in hand .The rose garden was Jim's
pride and joy, and he spent many unpaid hours
of his time tending, naturing and nurturing the
large, sweet smelling blooms. On this day they
wore a rather bedraggled air and looked as if
some light aircraft had landed on them.

What on earth has happened here, Jim I
asked.

"You may well hask ,professor" answered
Jim.

"Well, we 'ad a funeral in ere last week of a
nice old duck, and her son come along and 'ees
well cut up like. 'COS I mean losin' yer muvva is
an ard business at the best of times, like"

"So'ee says to me"Got a fag on yer mate? I understood, like, cos I mean losin' yer muvvah is an 'ard business like" So I 'as a feel in me pockets like , but no fags So I SAYS TO 'IM"Nip over the garage, cos they sells fags an'that there, so of 'ee goes like I sees 'im go into the garage and I CARRIES ON WIV ME GARDENIN' When 'ee comes back wiv a gallon petrol in a can like.

Professor I don't claim to be clairvoyant or nuffink, but something said to me, Watch out Jim, this bastard's going to play silly buggers in a minnit!

Hany way ;ee 'as got a fag in is mouft like, but'ee suddenly shouts out for'is muvvah and pours the whole can of juice all over 'imself like. WHOOSH! Suddenly 'ees like a 'uman Torch ""I SHOUTS, quick, Arry an' we'll chuck 'im in the fishpond like"

Me an 'Arry runs over to im , but 'ees like a 'yuman Guy Fox like the 'eat was so great we couldn't stick'im like. Any road our Graham appears and says "as'ow the Fire brigade are on their way"

They comes flying through the gates like general Custer, sees wats 'appened and lets fly with their strongest jet..It lifted up Guy Fox, and bowled him through my rose garden, and smashed the lot to fuck. Not content with that they then turns their water cannon on me an' 'Arry in case we are also alight like" The blast lifted me an' 'Arry straight into the bleed'n fishpond. Has yo know, professor 'Arry ain't a well man, an' 'ee was cryin' an'shakin' like I took the fellars off the fire engine to pull us out of the pond!"

I said to Jim, when my laughter had subsided, "Is Graham not in today, his car is not here and his office appears to be empty."Jim's face broke into a broad smile, LET ME HEXPLAIN MY DEAR OLD PROFESSOR. The habsences what you 'ave noticed are easily hexplained 'cos Red Knob 'as been fired like! Two mumfs ago we as 'ere a service for an M.E.P, a bit of a big knob like. So we all of us are on our best behaviour!

They was very precise about the music wot we was to play. Coming in we 'ad to play Hedward Helgars pomp and circumstance march,No.4 in Gmajor like, Then when we comes to the low ring they wants Hedward Helgars Nimrod. Going out they wants morning from Peer Gynt by Grieg,

"What happened? I hears you cry"!

They comes in to the Helgar and all O.K.but at the lowering no Nimrod, instead poor old 'Arry gets a bit flummoxed like and out comes The black Dyke Mills band playing THE TEDDY BEARS PICNIC. "Red faces all round! "At the going out no Grieg, We gets The Monty Python crahd singing ALWAYS LOOK ON THE BRIGHT SIDE OF LIFE!" SO EEES GORN FO GOOD!

The Organist's Revenge

One of the more frequent visitors to the crematorium was a local minister, a red haired Welshman called Mr Jones, We called him Jones the watch from his annoying habit of continually checking the time as if just being at this service was an annoying interruption in his calling of saving souls for Christ. It was a very expensive time piece made in Basle in Switzerland. I know all of this because I stole the watch and "popped" it at a Pawnbrokers, realising fifty pounds. I hurried back to the crematorium and finding the little cup hook upon which Mr. Jones habitually hung his watch I carefully hung the pawn ticket on the cup hook. Talk about "light the blue touch paper and retire to a safe distance. I looked

down from the organ console to see the fuzzy red hair and domed semi bald head of Mr Jones literally screaming, "JIM" at the very top of his voice. Jim appeared at the wretched mans elbow"nah then wot's up? your reverence.

"WHATS UP! SOMEONE'S PAWNED MY FUCKING WATCH!" I left it on here as I always do! and now look A BLOODY PAWN TICKET!" Jim said "ow much did they get for your old ticker?"

"SIXTY BLOODY QUID he roared Someone's got to pay see" he said in a voice cracking with emotion" That was my father's watch see boyo!" "Tell you what" said Jim "If I was you i'd get dahn that pawn shop a bit rapid like afore they sells it onto whoever comes in their shop and takes a fancy to it like"

OFF WENT HIS REVERENCE RED FACED AND AT HIGH SPEED.

Jim said: "IM OF ALL PEOPLE A BLEEDIN' PAWN TICKET"! WHEN HE comes back it would be a bloody good idea to be invisible like"

CRIPPLED with laughter: "Cos ee's going to want blood you can rest assured" Jim was choking with laughter, "'im of all people A bleedn' pawn ticket. So," gentlemen what we gonna do?" I walked slowly towards them dangling the missing watch by its strap

"Professor what HAVE you done? Asked Jim

"I have taught him a long overdue lesson, the pompous Welsh twunt" I replied.

Hardly had the words left my mouth when the chapel door burst open and HIS reverence rushed in ITS GONE!" he shrieked some other bastard's got it!

Jim all wide eyed innocence said "where you said you left this watch of yours?"

"On the hook where I always leave it" spat the Welshman.

"If are was you I would change my habits, your reverence laughed Jim"

"Try leaving it on your wrist!

That was positively the last we ever saw of the Reverent Jones. The tea room rocked with laughter for days afterwards and I was "accepted" as a member of their brotherhood.

Erroll's Farewell

As a freelance Minister one meets "all sorts and conditions of men"

The call came through from an East end Undertaker that a man named Erroll had just passed away and was I available to officiate at his burial service at Manor Park Cemetery on Friday morning at 11.30. I agreed and arranged to call on the grieving Widow to design Erroll's funeral. I met the by now distressed lady and her three children with whom I shared a mars bar.

Throughout the evening I heard of Erroll's great love of his wife and children. What a hard working provider he was to his family. Wedding photographs were produced; tears were shed and I left for home after promising that I would do my best and keep the service mercifully short. Fast forward! gentle reader to Friday morning Manor Park Cemetery on a hot, sunny morning. I Stood at the Chapel entrance chatting to a couple of gravediggers and the Chapel Master

"Ear Yar Squire, Yor lots ear nah" said the Chapel Master.

Entering the Main gates was an immaculate Austin Princess hearse bedecked with flowers spelling the word FARVIE, It purred up to the Chapel door and stopped.. Following this was an equally immaculate Austin Princess limousine containing the Widow and the three children, this too stopped behind the hearse.

Approaching the limousine I opened the rear door and reassured the widow that I would keep the proceedings as short as dignity allowed. Widow cried and the kids joined in so I shut the door to allow them some privacy in their grief.

It was then that I heard a very noisy car, snarling its way towards us at an unseemly speed. It screeched to a halt and the driver a fat man in a tight fitting blue suit emerged and shambled menacingly towards me massaging his enormous right fist with his fat left hand. Thrusting his bucolic face into mine, treating me to an unwelcome miasma of last night's beer he growled; "Nna ven wots all vis ere ven YOU'VE UPSET MY MISSIS YOU' AVE"

The passenger door of the little red car crashed shut, and hurrying towards me was a rather slatternly looking woman hefting her shoulder bag into place. "EAR WHY AVENT YO COME TO SEE ME" She screamed. I murmered "Perhaps you could inform me as to why I should have seen you"

"COS IM IS BLEEDIN' WIFE INN I?" SHE SPAT.

"YER IS BLEEDIN WIFE " echoed TIGHT BLUE SUIT.

I walked determinedly toward the waiting room into which they followed me.

"WOT WE IN EAR FOR rumbled blue suit.

"I want to explain a rather unfortunate mistake", I bleated. "MAKE IT GOOD Padre overwise I'm gonna smash yor effin face in". He then punched his left hand with his great right fist with truly horrifying force.

"Behind the hearse is a car containing a Lady with three children. She purports to be Erroll's wife and moreover to be the mother of his three children".

"SHE F F*CKIN WHAT? " SHE ROARED AT A VOLUME THAT MUST SURELY HAVE REGISTERED A SEVEN ON THE RICHTER SCALE AND BEEN CLEARLY AUDIBLE IN Romford Market.

A nervous cough sounded and the Chapel Master said ,"May we please proceed with the service 'Mr Saxton' As you can imagine I needed no second bidding"

I: "Please Ladies and gentlemen make your way into the Chapel"

I positioned myself at the head of the coffin and began. "I am the resurrection and I am the life said the LORD, He that live and believeth in me shall never die". I mounted into the Pulpit and noticed that several members of the congregation were heavily handcuffed to Prison Officers on either side of them.

One of whom appeared to be a friend of blue suit who shouted: "Awright Chawley?" and waved a greeting. My old friend and mentor Jim Rivers voice sounded ghostlike in my ear. "Take my tip professor and git aht of ere as quick as you like, SOON AS 'IS CAWFIN 'ITS THE GROUND, do your earth to earth bit and be of like a Jewish Fore skin. Cos this lot looks well handy and they're here for a rumble like, So do yourself a big favour and fuck of sharpish."

THE SERVICE CAME TO AN END AND WE PROGRESSED WITH Erroll's body to the hearse. I was given a box of earth by M ICHAEL the Undertaker. "Michael", I said: "This daft bugger's got two wives neither of whom knows of the others existence".

"Aw fookin ell' said Michael, What are you going to do?"

"Large lumps of f*ck all," I SAID with great feeling. The journey was like a march to the Scaffold, I positioned myself with my box of earth at the head of the grave. Up staggered the bearers with Erroll's body. Several fights had broken out by this time I could see blue suit doing terrible things to people with his knees and he and "Chawley" punching all and sundry.

'For as much as it hath pleased Almighty God to take unto himself the soul of our beloved brother Erroll we commit his body to the ground earth to earth sprinkle, sprinkle 'Ashes to Ashes' SPRINKLE, SPRINKLE 'and Dust to dust'. 'In sure and certain hope of the resurrection to Eternal life through our Lord Jesus Christ'. At this juncture I passed the Ornamental box of earth to my right straight into the fat hands of Tight Blue Suit who promptly threw it into the face of a Lady opposite him.

I HAVE NEVER SEEN A Lady goalkeeper! If you ever need one please telephone as I know just the Lady that you need.

With truly balletic grace this lady caught the speeding box when but inches from her face and twirling on her high heels and assuming the stance of a Discus Thrower, she hurled the box with stunning force full into the fat face of blue suit

IT HIT HIS MOUTH or as he would say MOUFT WITH Stunning force.

"AAAAAAAAAARRRRGGGGGGGGGHH HHHH". He cried and falling, slid down the outside of the grave mound into the roadway where I had conveniently parked my car.

This was my Golden moment. Sliding down, I leapt for the roadway. In advertantly treading on a fat white hand. The silence of the quiet graveyard; the Yew trees shade where lies the earth in many a mouldering heap, was shattered with the roar of "YOOO BARSTURD".

I ran for the door of my car, scrabbling frantically for my keys. I opened the door and lifting my robes up around my waist I slammed the door shut and locked myself in. 'Gott sei

Gedank' the car fired first go and I was away heading for the exit.

I then noticed Blue suit REDIVIVUS running through the graveyard to cut off my escape running diagonally across the graveyard hurdling gravestones for all the world like a fat Ed. Moses.

AS I DREW LEVEL WITH HIM HIS LEADING HURDLINGLEG CLIPPED A GRAVESTONE WHICH BROUGHT HIS GREAT FAT BODY CRASHING DOWN ONTO THE NEXT GRAVE WHICH HAD AN IRON KERBING; I WAS FREE!

When I ARRIVED HOME, Friederike sat me in my favourite armchair with a glass of Brandy and my two cats Bonnie and Molly to calm me down. I telephoned Michael and enquired as to the end of the 'Schmeer'. "Police took a load of them away and the bloke in the blue suit had a nasty mess where his face used to be".

Farewell Joe Strummer. Number One Not One Of A Number

This meant a very long car journey on a Saturday since living on my boat and writing full time I have developed the habit of dinning out on Friday evenings, lying in on Saturdays driving into Cambridge to attend Synagogue. So this Saturday was going to be very different. I drove out to the village garage and filled my Morgan to the brim. I checked the oil, water and battery levels and motored back to my mooring for an early night, the forecast for the West Country was far from promising! gales, floods were the very least of it. I telephoned Mrs Strummer and asked for directions. "Come into Bridgewater" she said ; take the main left fork and you will come to a Land Rover garage, meet me there" I travelled down the M11 to the M25 and around to the M30, a sentimental journey as when I had a family I had a HOLIDAY HOME IN A Cornish village named Trebarwith Strand, and we frequently drove along this well remembered road. Reaching Bridgewater in torrential rain I quickly located the Land Rover garage and there I met Mrs Strummer in her Volvo estate car, we proceeded slowly and carefully along flooded lanes, it was like driving along a not so shallow river After some time we turned into the driveway of Joe Strummers' farmhouse, a delightful old farmhouse set in the Mendip Hills.

We all sat around a large oak traditional farmhouse table Next to an open log fire and spoke of the many facets of JOE Strummer's life. What a vibrant and invigorating person he was to work with, of his great friendship with Nelson Mandela, how the last song Joe Strummer wrote was dedicated to Nelson Mandela and whose title was in fact Mandela's prison number whilst he spent twenty seven years in Robben Island prison. The band recorded this song on the roof of Robben Island.

I met some of Joe's best friends especially one, Dick Rude. Dick contributed totally brilliantly to Joe's Eulogy on the day of his funeral. Time wore on and I HAD RELUCTANTLY TO TAKE MY LEAVE OF THESE DELIGHTFUL PEOPLE, I decided to use the M4, "Well, the rain and floods were definitely getting worse as I headed for the fens, James" end my way home via the M4, much, much quicker

I arrived in the Boathaven at 12.30 feeling worn out and ready for my bed I had my nightly conversation with my imaginary footman, one JAMES" good evening your Grace, I am glad to see you safe home, how was your journey?" Bob said that the forecast for the West of England was frightful" "I decided to wend my way home thought that using the M4 James ,so much quicker you know"

"Will you partake of you evening brandy, "my Lord?

"Funnily enough James I poured myself a balloon before I left this morning so I will enjoy that and so to bed James" "Very good your grace "said James:"Shall we give the boat a good battery run tomorrow, my lord" said James. "Yes James, I thought that we might like to venture out into the Wash and to dine at that fish place, at Wells next the sea" O wonderful my lord!" I do so enjoy going there"! James bowed, "Good night my Lord," "Good night James, see you in the morning"

I sat in the wheelhouse sipping my Brandy and reflecting on life generally, David and Carole arrived home from their meal in Browns restaurant in Cambridge. I was glad to see that they were now an "item" David had spent most of last week painting up her little narrow boat, in Kelvin Green and very smart it looked too. I wish them well; to love and be loved is the most important of the Eternal One's gifts. I moved into my boardroom and switching on my computer I began writing Joe Strummer's Eulogy. Joe, whom Heaven bless, was born into a "top drawer family, his parents were in the diplomatic service, with all that implies, one got the distinct impression that Joe had been expected to follow suit and that Mater and Pater were unimpressed with having a pop star as their son. The bloody fools! Joe added so much to the world through his music, through his innate integrity and his enormous gift of friendship which transcended all barriers of caste, religion, musical taste and race Joe Strummer was as near as I shall ever get to a SAINT! His friends, of whom Nelson Mandela was one, adored Joe and held him in utter respect on the day of the funeral the entire chapel was full to overflowing, even filling the large atrium.

We broadcast his service through enormous speakers so that all of his thousands of fans who were standing silently in the rain, could hear. We played his songs from London calling which even I KNEW! Many were crying, not loudly to gain attention, just real tears rolling down their cheeks. They genuinely loved Joe Strummer.

As you know by now, gentle reader, I am a Jew, so I began Joe's service with the ringing words from the Talmud DEATH, IS NOT AND NEVER CAN BE THE END OF LIFE. I DO NOT BELIEVE IN DEATH

All the while we hold Joe in our memory, speak of him, remembering all his many successes ,his gift of friendship to folks of all races, creeds and colours. Then Joe transcends death. I DO NOT BELIEVE IN DEATH! One of the guests at the service was Patrick Moore, the Astronomer, I have been an amateur astronomer for years and now that I live on my boat in the Fenlands I often spend my time with a telescope up in the flying bridge of stolen hours" watching the slowly expanding universe, and being lost in the sheer wonder of the planets. Patrick who simply fizzes with enthusiasm promised to visit me and see for himself, on saying which he explained that his sight was beginning to fail, and would I do him the honour of visiting him at his observatory and use his giant telescope. SO, thank you Joe Strummer, without you that could never have happened. YOU MADE IT HAPPEN, and I am so grateful, as I said I DO NOT BELIEVE IN DEATH!

The end Hildesheim 2007

Pick Of The Week and Later Radio 4's Pick of the Year.

Len had dropped right out of society. No official name no numbers, nothing to identify this child of God. For a week or two, then one day the car is taken from you. You, go home by bus, your wife has interrupted a call from the bank or the mortgage company threatening to repossess your home and pretend that all is well you set off for work in your company car dressed as you always are for business.

The authorities had tried long, hard and diligently to trace any family or friends of Len, but o no avail to all intents and purposes Len had disappeared. I said to the pitifully small congregation not hat had assembled for Len "Do not sit here feeling safe and superior to Len. YOU HAVE DOUBTLESSLY ENJOYED A NICE BREAKFAST AND HOT COFFEE. You TRUST THAT AT THE END OF THE MONTH YOUR SALARY WILL EXCEED YOU OUTGOINGS

AND THAT YOU PROVIDE YOUR WIFE AND FAMILY WITH SECURITY" Don't be so easily fooled. Security is often a dilution. What happened to Len can happen to any tone. You go into work one day to find that your firm has been taken over by a business rival. In the "rationalisation which inevitably follows your department and your job is axed. You try and pretend to your wife and family that all is well, you leave at the same time each day for work, but spend your day in the public library trying to find a job. Your wife after a nasty call from the bank or building society gathers the kids to her and leaves home to live with her mother.

You have lost your family and those dearest to you! Being a minister is very hard on occasions, I think of a pop song entitled "streets of London, "The chorus of which says:

So don't you tell me you're lonely a
And life to you has been unkind!
Let me take you b y the hand,
and lead you through the streets of London
I'll show you something that'll
make you change your mind!

A Horl Ob His Orn!!

I was instructed to officiate at the funeral of Uncle Rufus at Manor Park Cemetery. I was warned that as the family were short of money that Rufus's brothers had opted that his body should be buried in what is termed a common grave. I should explain that to dig a single grave costs many thousands of pounds, whereas the common grave is else actively cheap and saves extremely valuable burial space.

The common grave is dug to a depth of some 35 feet, and coffins are deposited one resting on the other until the grave is full. Some folk find this practice objectionable and it is best to gloss over the practice until after the service and the interment. I went to meet the family and was straight away informed that their Uncle Rufus was a very important man who posed a GOLD WATCH, and had risen to the high position of a collector for a large insurance company. During their explanation and history of their uncle, by a slip of the tongue I referred to him as Uncle REMUS.

This caused an explosion of wrath from The hearse purred up to me bearing the message spelt out in flowers NUMBER ONE, NOT ONE OF A NUMBER! Auntie Primrose his last was a truly Amazonian lady with arms as muscular as a steel scaffolding erector and two of the largest breasts that I HAVE EVER SEEN.

The left one made one think of Saint Paul's cathedral on its side! She said "Now then Farder this here, is a big important man it ain't no Walt Disney time here his name is RUFUS NOT REMUS" So saying she rose to her sandalled feet and stumped off showing a derriere as large as that of a grass blown horse.

On the way back home I noticed that Michaels lights were on and that he was still working, so I POPPED IN TO HAVE A WORD. Michael:"Do this family really know what a commons grave is?"

"Not really, said Michael, but they understands the money that is saved"

With a heart full of foreboding I arrived at Manor Park, wandering over to the section set aside for commons burials I mounted the grave mound and looked down. The depth was horrifying dark and seemingly bottomless! The gravediggers had as always done their best by covering the lower coffin with a generous layer of vine leaves which helped to mask the stark reality. Even so it was with a heart full of trepidation that I went into the robbing room and donned the robes of righteousness. We walked on at snails' pace and had almost reached the grave when BANG, the front bum they arrived in their hundreds from coaches and cars. THE HEARSE PURRED UP TO ME SPELLING out in flowers the message NUMBER ONE NOT ONE OF A NUMBER.

During the service in the chapel I continually emphasised THAT Uncle Rufus was a big, big man nods of Approval all round "He rose to the heights of a collector for the Standard an insurance group "yeah! dat raaaaght farder" from Auntie Primrose: And of course you will all of you recall with pride his wonderful gold watch which he was awarded by his grateful company. A welter of clapping and cheering broke out, and I felt that perhaps, if I was lucky all would come right Rufus's body was carried out of the chapel and loaded back onto the hearse. We began our march to the graveside Michael said" watch your back down here, Malcolm, we've got that stupid bloody Andy driving again today, the little bastard ran me over yesterday, he said that his foot went into a spasm. I'll give him spasm IF HE EVER DOES IT AGAIN, SILLY LITTLE SOD"

We carried on at a snails' pace and had almost reached the grave, when BANG, the front bumper of the hearse connected with the back of my knees and I went sprawling in a heap. I laid supine in the mud and leaves until I found myself lifted as if by a crane and dumped onto my feet Auntie Primrose had observed my fall and gripping me by the rope girdled had one handedly lifted me. She rounded on Andy the unfortunate young driver "Look what you have done to poor farder. " I Shook my head "My old knee has given out after my fall ", I groaned, so we went on with the interment but it was a bad moment!

He roared, you stooped KONT he can hardly walk now thanks to you and unleashed a truly wonderful impression of a Vulcan Death punch. Andy went down and lay there writhing. I was sorely tempted to join him as I saw the accident as what could be my "blighty ticket, absolving me from any further participation in what I WAS

SURE WAS GOING TO TURN INTO A RIGHT
BARNEY

Enter Auntie Primrose

"Now look here farder dis ennt right enntitt"
she screamed." HE WANTS A HORL OB HIS
ORN! Dat dere hole is already full ob dead
buggers enntitt!" I looked desperately around
for Michael but saw him sitting in the hearse,
engaged in earnest conversation that brooked no
interruption.

Auntie Primrose returned with several shovels
in her fat hands "Now den farder we can start

digging a proper horl for Rufus enntit she
menaced" I shook my head , My old knee has
given out after my fall I groaned. She was far
from impressed "You can't leave here now, not
until we interred Rufus" Uncle's never going to
rest without a horl ob his orn!"

The Cemetery manager was called for and
they all retired into his office to argue things
out.

Upon their return we were faced with a
curious situation. They had decided that rather
than subject Uncle Rufus to the ignominy of a
common burial, they had all contributed to his
body being cremated, so that was alright then!

We entered the crematorium chapel and I said the final prayers of committal for Rufus and left a much relieved minister!

Is this all there is? Or does life go on??? This as a Minister is the most asked question in my job.

To answer this in any religious sense is almost impossible in terms of the Church of England one can only say of that institution "It is a true religion but it is NOT THE TRUTH!"

I am a practising Jew and one of the basic tenets of Judaism says "Death is not and never can be the end of life". We have to consider that all of us and those we love are made up of body and soul or spirit. The body dies sooner or later but our souls transcend this experience we have only to look at nature to appreciate the metamorphosis of death. In your garden every year caterpillars die and change into butterflies, death being for them, merely a change! As I AM convinced that it is for all of us living creatures, it is the Grand design of the Great Architect of the Universe, at whose creative Fiat all things first were made THE creative light brings us back to Kabbalah, the mystical dimension of Judaism the study of which allows us, intellectually to bridge the chasm between life and death.

Does it really work? I am often asked. The stunning answer to this is YES! The power of your love and the power of your combined intellect can bridge the gap of parting and allow you both to "touch souls" Just empty your mind and present your loved one with a clean page to write their message on. This is not strictly spiritualism, this is practical Judaism!

If when you were a tiny baby in your mother's womb I had told you, that three inches away from you was another world with light, colour and your life's love awaiting you.

You would never have believed a word that was said to you. You'd have said "Leave of!"MY WORLD IS IN HERE AND I am just fine I'm fed , warm loved and protected. I don't want to go anywhere, I'm more than happy here, and I DON'T BELIEVE THAT THIS WORLD OF YOURS EXISTS"!!!

The Diver

I had notice diver particularly from the first moment. A girl in glasses, extremely and quite naturally upset. As we entered the chapel she began to advance on her knees behind the coffin, stopping occasionally to genuflect and to cross herself murmuring strings of unintelligible words, gazing upwards to the chapel ceiling as if seeing beatific visions

She appeared an ardent Catholic and as I thought she joined in the Our Father and the Hail Mary with a fervent gusto we arranged ourselves in a half circle. The young lady approached me and enquired of my box of earth as to whether it had been blessed. I replied in the affirmative, where upon she plunged her hand into the box and, taking a large handful she promptly ate it!

Hallo, hallo I thought we've got a right one here!

I moved to the head of the grave and began the words of committal

`For as much as it has pleased Almighty God to take unto Himself the soul of our sister Avril, we now commit her body to the ground, earth to earth, ashes to ashes and dust to dust, insure and certain hope of the resurrection to eternal life through our Lord Jesus Christ`. And then, came a high pitched scream and a cry of "I'M COMING WITH YOU MUVVER!" AND DOWN SHE PLUNGED BANGING HER FACE ON THE COFFIN LID AND HURTING HERSELF CONSIDERABLY. What could I have done? I ASKED MYSELF. If I had stood next to her and attempted to exercise some form of restraint I might well have found myself in the bottom of the grave too and facing a charge of assault to boot!

They really should pay us danger money you know

The perils are many and varied

We were at EAST London Cemetery and the service had progressed smoothly. At the graveside all was well until we came to lowered the coffin into the grave. In short the coffin was too large for the hole that had been prepared. The temptation as a minister to put your foot on the coffin lid is immense, you feel that all it would take is one determined kick and all would be well.

Oh no! the JCB digger has to be summoned and we all have to withdraw with the mourners, say a few extra prayers until the digger has clanked its way to the graveside, extended its bucket dug down, and lifted a great chunk of fresh earth. This of course renders the newly dug grave resembling "hill 60 in the first world war. Result tears all round, loud sniffs and a few sharp words of remonstranc to the minister!

I can assure you that a minister's lot is not a happy one. Folks at funerals are often very angry that their loved one has, as they say been taken. They are angry with God, but of course God is safely tucked away in His Heaven and therefore well out of reach, so they pick on the next best thing, to wit the poor sod of a minister. And don't they just!

Within most families a funeral represents a financial crisis with members of the extended family having to contribute towards the cost with little prospect of any financial recompense.

Such was the case with Billy Steele. Billy's old Grannie 'ad pegged it like an' 'is fat slag of a sister 'ad fahnd out as 'ow Billy had trousered two fahsend pahnd bonus and was flush like'.

They come a' knocking at Billy's door one night to remind him of his good fortune and as 'ow they were all well Boracic like Boracic, gentle reader is short for boracic lint which is cockney rhyming slang for `skint` i.e. to have no money. Corse Billy does 'is nut like', calls 'is sister a fat slag an' a greedy CAH!`

Which prompts sister's husband`Chawley` to issue a warning to Billy to `watch 'is mouft! in case he, Chawley would offer Billy a `knuckle sandwich` to which Billy riposted with reminding` Chawley` as 'ow 'is` muvver` was the biggest old whore in the entire East end of London, and `poxed up` to boot.

I went round to make a pastoral visit to the family with this monumental row still blazing around me. Billy insisting that when grannies house was sold that he, and no other should be the principal beneficiary, certainly not his sister or that lazy `git` `Chawley`who, couldn't hold a job down for more than a week! Sister pipes up with "she promised me as 'ow I could 'ave ' er washing machine promised me that on 'er death bed she did` Billy roared` Listen you greedy cah all wot she 'ad is being sold like until I gets my bonus back` I worked my `bollocks` off for that money 'an' I'M 'AVIN IT back like" In this mood we departed for the cemetery where ,on arrival we were to sing the hymn" Make me a channel of your peace! I thought, FAT CHANCE! The flower bedecked hearse pulled up outside the cemetery chapel and out climbed the driver Len ,he pointed to an enormous scratch on the flanks of the hearse and an accompanying broken window

"I tell you that Billy's a NANIMAL!" I gets rahnd Clegg Street and 'im an' Chawley are aht in the street punchin' fuck aht of each uvver!" I called to mind that Billy Steele had won the light heavy weightA BA title recently at the Albert Hall! Grannies body was carried into the chapel and her service began. Loud sniffs and wails from sister, but of BILLY, NO SIGN.` Chawley` approached sporting a truly magnificent black eye`Billy ain't comin' FARVER, cos 'ees got the right ump`.

I concluded the service by saying "and now, in peace let us take grannie's body to rest with that of her husband of forty years Bert plonker his name it turned out was PLOWRIGHT but it really did look like Plonker on the burial form! After the burial of granny we all packed ourselves back into the funeral cars for our return to grannies home in Clegg Street I sat with Len in the scratched and broken windowed hearse. As we got to Clegg Street, our way was blocked by an enormous pantechnicon,we waited until it lumbered round the corner freeing our entry Unfortunately our way was again blocked by an even larger pantechnicon being driven by none other than the light heavy weight Billy Steele, sporting a bloodied nose As we edged past him he waved a thumbs up and shouted! AWRIGHT MATE? Len and the rest of the mourners entered grannies old home to be met by a tearful neighbour who enquired as to our wants. Her voice seemed to raise a curious echo effect. Looking around I quickly realised why the house was entirely empty ;no carpets, no curtains, no chairs, no beds, and NO WASHING MACHINE.

As Len said to me "you don't need Sherlock bleedin' Holmes to tell you where that lot's gone

It's probably being sold dahn the market even as we speak"! acknowledged.